An Introduction to Search Engine Optimisation

A SIMPLE GUIDE TO EFFECTIVE SEO FOR WEBSITE OWNERS AND MANAGERS

J.M. Chittick

An Introduction to Search Engine Optimisation

A simple guide to effective SEO for website owners and managers

An Introduction to Search Engine Optimisation

A simple guide to effective SEO for website owners and managers

J.M. Chittick

Contents

1. Introduction to SEO

1.1. Definition and importance of SEO in digital marketing

Search Engine Optimisation (commonly known as SEO) is a way to ensure that your website appears high up on search engine results pages so that your site will get more visitors who actually want to be there. Big organisations spend a lot of time and money ensuring that their website appears at or near the very top of search engine results pages. I'm guessing, if you are reading this book, that you do not have the huge budget or staff of bigger organisations and you want a simple and straightforward guide for understanding and implementing search engine optimisation on your website? This guide has been written for those who want to quickly understand and get to grips with the basics of SEO and take practical steps to implement SEO to improve the search engine results of their website. Longer, more detailed books about SEO are available and this book is not trying to compete with them in terms of detail or completeness.

Search Engine Optimisation (SEO) is a fundamental component of digital marketing that focuses on enhancing a website's visibility in organic (non-paid) search engine results. It encompasses a range of strategies, techniques, and practices aimed at improving the ranking and appearance of web pages in search engines like Google, Bing, and Yahoo. The primary goal of SEO is to increase a website's relevance and authority for specific keywords and phrases to attract more visitors from the target audience for that website.

The importance of SEO in digital marketing can be summarised as:

1. Increased Visibility and Traffic

SEO helps improve a website's rankings in search engine results pages (SERPs), making it more visible to potential visitors. A higher ranking will typically lead to more website traffic, as users are more likely to click on the top results.

2. Cost-Effectiveness

Unlike paid advertising, the traffic generated through organic search results does not have a cost per click or impression – the cost comes from the time someone takes in making a website more search engine friendly. This makes SEO an efficient and cost-effective strategy for driving traffic, in the long term, to a website.

3. Credibility and Trust

Websites that appear higher in search results are often perceived as more trustworthy and credible by users. SEO helps build your website's and, by extension, your brand's authority and reputation online.

4. Enhanced User Experience

SEO involves optimising the structure, navigation, and content of a website, making it more user-friendly. A well-optimised site can provide a better experience, encouraging visitors to stay longer and interact more with the content.

5. Competitive Advantage

By optimising their website more effectively than their competitors, organisations can achieve higher rankings, attract more targeted traffic, and gain a competitive advantage in their industry or sector.

6. Targeted Marketing

SEO strategies are typically centred on keywords that the target audience may use to search for products or services. This ensures that the traffic coming to the site is more likely to be interested in what the website offers, leading to higher user conversion rates.

7. Adaptability to Market Changes

SEO strategies can be adapted and updated in response to changes in user behaviour, market trends, and algorithm updates by search engines. This adaptability makes it a vital component of an ongoing and dynamic digital marketing strategy.

8. Measurable Results

With tools like Google Analytics and Google Search Console, organisations can track the performance of their SEO efforts, including traffic, rankings, and conversions. This data allows for informed decisions and strategy adjustments when considering future SEO (or general marketing) plans.

SEO is a critical element of digital marketing that not only helps to improve a website's visibility and user experience but also contributes to building the credibility and authority of a brand in the online world. Its cost-effectiveness and ability to help organisations target specific audiences, make it an indispensable strategy for businesses aiming to thrive online.

1.2. Overview of how search engines work

Understanding how search engines work is fundamental to mastering search engine optimisation (SEO). At their basic level, search engines aim to provide users with the most relevant and authoritative results for their queries. The process involves three main steps: crawling, indexing, and ranking.

1. Crawling

Crawling is the first step, where search engines use bots (also known as spiders or crawlers) to discover publicly available webpages. These bots start with a list of web addresses from past crawls and sitemaps provided by website owners. As they visit these URLs, they use the links found on these pages to discover other pages. This process allows the bots to find new content and updates to existing content quickly.

2. Indexing

Once a page is discovered, the search engine tries to understand what that page is about — this process is known as indexing. During indexing, the content of the page is analysed to determine its topics and other key elements (like images, videos, and other media) that might influence its relevance to specific search queries. The search engine processes and stores this information in a huge database, called the index, so it can be quickly retrieved when needed.

3. Ranking

Ranking is the final step, where pages are ordered in the search results based on their relevance and authority for a specific query. When a user performs a search, the search engine sifts through its index to provide the best answers to the query. It uses complex, constantly changing, algorithms that consider hundreds of ranking factors, such as the use of relevant keywords, the quality of content, user engagement metrics, page speed, inbound links and so on. The goal is to provide users with a list of pages that best answer their query, ordered by most to least relevant.

Key Factors Influencing Search Engine Operations:

- Algorithms: Search engines use proprietary algorithms to assess and rank webpages. These algorithms are updated frequently to improve the relevance and quality of results.
- Relevance: Determines how well a webpage's content matches the searcher's query, considering factors like the presence of search keywords in titles, headings, and body content.
- Authority: Assesses the webpage's credibility, often through the quality and quantity of other websites that link to it. High-quality inbound links suggest the content is trustworthy and valuable.
- User Experience: Search engines also consider signals that indicate a good user experience, such as mobile-friendliness, ease of navigation, and fast loading times.
- Security: Websites that use secure protocols (HTTPS) are often favoured in search results, as they provide a safer browsing experience.

Search engines continuously evolve, refining their algorithms to better serve the needs of the user and adapt to new technologies and web standards. Keeping up with these changes is critical for SEO practitioners to optimise websites effectively for search visibility.

1.3. The difference between organic vs. paid results

The distinction between organic and paid search results is crucial in understanding how search engine results pages (SERPs) work and formulating an effective digital marketing strategy. Here's a breakdown of the key differences:

Organic Search Results

- Definition: Organic search results are listings on search engine results pages that appear because of their relevance to the search terms, as opposed to their being advertisements. Search engines use complex algorithms to determine the order of these results.
- Cost: There is no <u>direct</u> cost to appear in organic search results. Rankings are achieved through SEO efforts that focus on optimising website content, structure, and off-site factors like backlinks.
- Credibility and Trust: Many users trust organic results more than ads because they are determined by relevance to their search query rather than the budget behind them.

- Effort and Time: Achieving a high ranking in organic search results can take considerable time and requires ongoing SEO efforts. The process involves optimising content, improving site speed, ensuring mobile-friendliness, and acquiring quality backlinks, among other strategies. So, by its very nature, should mean better search results for the user.
- Long-term Value: While it takes longer to see results from SEO, the benefits are more sustainable over time. A well-optimised site can maintain its position in search results with continued effort, providing a steady stream of traffic.

Paid Search Results

- Definition: Paid search results are advertisements that appear on search engine results pages. Advertisers pay to have their ads shown for specific keywords, and these ads are usually marked with an "Ad" label to distinguish them from organic results.
- Cost: Paid search operates on a pay-per-click (PPC) model, meaning advertisers pay each time someone clicks on their ad. The cost per click varies depending on the competitiveness of the keyword and quality score of the ad.
- Immediate Visibility: Paid search provides immediate visibility and can be an effective way to generate traffic quickly, especially for new websites/businesses or those not ranking well organically.
- Targeting and Flexibility: Paid ads allow for more precise targeting, including by geography, language, device, and time of day. Campaigns can be adjusted in real-time based on performance.
- Measurement and Analysis: PPC platforms provide detailed metrics on ad performance, including impressions, clicks, and conversions, allowing advertisers to measure their return on investment (ROI) effectively and make data-driven decisions.

Key Differences Summarised

- Visibility: Paid results can provide immediate visibility, while organic results are achieved over time through effective SEO activity and decisions.
- Cost: Organic search traffic is free, while paid search requires a budget for ads.
- Trust: Organic results may carry more credibility with users, as they are earned through relevance and authority rather than paid placements.
- Sustainability: Organic rankings can provide long-term benefits, while paid search is dependent on on-going financial investment.
- Control and Targeting: Paid search offers more control over when and where ads appear and who sees them, along with easier measurement of return on investment.

Both organic and paid search have their place in a comprehensive digital marketing strategy, and many businesses find the most success by utilising both approaches to maximise visibility and drive traffic.

2. Keyword Research

2.1. Understanding keyword intent and how it influences content strategy

Understanding keyword intent is pivotal in shaping an effective content strategy, as it aligns the content with the users' needs and search behaviours, ultimately influencing conversions, engagement, and SEO success. Keyword intent refers to the purpose behind a search query - what the user intends to find or achieve when they type their query into a search engine. It can be broadly categorised into four main types:

1. Informational Intent

Description: Users are looking for information or answers to questions. These queries often start with "how," "what," "why," "when," or who."

Content Strategy: To target these queries, create informative and educational content like blog posts, guides, FAQs, and tutorials. The goal here is to provide valuable information that satisfies the searcher's curiosity or solves their problem.

2. Navigational Intent

Description: The searcher is looking for a specific website or page. They already have a destination in mind, such as "Facebook login" or the BBC homepage.

Content Strategy: For brands, it's essential to optimise the homepage and other key landing pages with clear branding and direct information. Ensure your site is easily navigable for users and search engines alike to facilitate quick access to sought-after pages.

3. Transactional Intent

Description: Users are ready to buy or are very close to making a purchase decision. These searches might include specific product names or terms like "buy," "deal," "discount," "price," or "for sale."

Content Strategy: Focus on creating content that facilitates the buying process, such as product pages, reviews, comparisons, and sales pages. Include clear calls-to-action (CTAs) and streamline the purchase process to convert these ready-to-buy users.

4. Commercial Investigation

Description: These searchers are considering a purchase and are looking for information to help them compare and decide. They might use terms like "best," "top," "review," or "comparison."

Content Strategy: Develop content that helps users make informed decisions, such as comprehensive comparison guides, expert reviews, and testimonials. Highlighting unique selling points (USPs) and differentiators can also sway users in favour of your product or service.

5. Influencing Content Strategy

Understanding the intent behind keywords allows content creators and marketers to tailor their content strategy to meet the users' needs effectively:

- Match Content with Intent: Ensure that the type of content you create (informative, navigational, transactional, or commercial) aligns with the intent behind the keywords you're targeting. This alignment increases the likelihood of engaging the audience and fulfilling their search needs.
- Improve User Experience and Engagement: By delivering content that resonates with the searcher's intent, you're more likely to provide a positive user experience, keep visitors on your site longer, and encourage them to undertake the desired actions.
- Enhance SEO Performance: Content that closely matches keyword intent is more likely to rank higher in search engine results pages (SERPs) because it's seen as more relevant to the searcher's needs. This can lead to increased visibility, more organic traffic, and higher engagement rates.
- Increase Conversion Rates: When content meets the user's intent, visitors are more likely to convert, whether that means making a purchase, signing up for a newsletter, or another desired action. Tailoring content to the various stages of the buyer's journey can guide users from awareness to decision-making more effectively.

In summary, understanding and exploiting keyword intent, is a critical component of any content strategy, enhancing both user satisfaction and content performance across search engines

2.2. Tools and techniques for effective keyword research

Effective keyword research is fundamental to a successful SEO strategy, helping to identify the terms and phrases your target audience is searching for. This insight allows you to tailor your content, products, and services to meet the needs of your audience. Here's an overview of tools and techniques that can aid in conducting thorough keyword research:

Tools for Keyword Research

1. Google Keyword Planner

Description: Primarily designed for advertising, it also provides valuable data on search volume, competition, and seasonal trends for keywords.

Benefits: Free to use with a Google Ads account; integrates directly with Google's vast data on search.

2. SEMrush

Description: A comprehensive SEO tool that offers detailed keyword research, including search volume, keyword difficulty, and variations.

Benefits: Provides insights into competitors' keyword strategies; useful for both organic and paid search research.

3. Ahrefs

Description: Another all-in-one SEO tool that excels in backlink analysis and keyword research, offering data on keyword difficulty, search volume, and SERP analysis.

Benefits: Great for finding content gaps and new keyword opportunities; offers a detailed view of the search landscape.

4. Moz Keyword Explorer

Description: Offers keyword suggestions, SERP analysis, and search volume data, with unique metrics like organic CTR and priority scores for keywords.

Benefits: User-friendly interface; integrates well with other Moz tools for a comprehensive SEO strategy.

5. Ubersuggest

Description: A free tool by Neil Patel that provides keyword suggestions, search volume data, and content ideas.

Benefits: Easy to use and offers valuable insights for beginners without a subscription.

6. AnswerThePublic

Description: Visualises search questions and suggested autocomplete searches in an image called a search cloud.

Benefits: Excellent for uncovering long-tail keywords and understanding the questions your audience is asking.

Techniques for Keyword Research

1. Analyse Competitors

Look at the keywords your competitors are targeting in their content and SEO efforts. Tools like SEMrush and Ahrefs can show you what keywords are driving traffic to your competitors' sites.

2. Use Google Autocomplete

Start typing a term in Google's search box, and note the autocomplete suggestions. These are often reflective of the most common searches related to your initial query.

3. Consider Search Intent

As you compile keywords, categorise them by search intent (informational, navigational, transactional, or commercial investigation) to ensure your content aligns with what searchers are looking for.

4. Leverage Long-Tail Keywords

Focus on long-tail keywords (more specific, often longer queries) as they tend to have lower competition and higher conversion rates.

5. Monitor Search Trends

Use Google Trends to identify and capitalise on trending topics or keywords. This can help you attract more traffic during peak interest periods.

6. Refine and Expand Your List

Regularly update and expand your keyword list based on performance data, emerging trends, and new products or services. SEO is an ongoing process, and your keyword strategy should evolve accordingly.

Combining these tools and techniques will give you a very solid foundation for understanding your audience's search behaviour, identifying keyword opportunities, and optimising your content for better search engine visibility.

Short-tail vs. long-tail keywords

Understanding the distinction between long-tail and short-tail keywords is crucial for formulating an effective SEO and content marketing strategy. Each type serves different user intents, competition levels, and conversion rates, impacting how you should target your audience.

Short-Tail Keywords

Definition: Short-tail keywords, also known as "head terms," are search phrases that are usually one to two words long. They are very broad and generic.

Characteristics

High Search Volume: These keywords have a high search volume because they are broad and cover a wide range of topics.

High Competition: Due to their broad nature, many websites compete to rank for these keywords, making it more challenging to secure top positions in search engine results pages (SERPs).

Lower Conversion Rates: While they can drive a significant amount of traffic, the traffic is often less targeted, leading to lower conversion rates compared to long-tail keywords.

Examples: "shoes", "books", "coffee".

Long-Tail Keywords

Definition: Long-tail keywords are longer phrases, typically three words or more, that are more specific than short-tail keywords. They often resemble short sentences or questions.

Characteristics

Lower Search Volume: These keywords have a lower search volume because they are more specific, targeting niche audiences or topics.

Lower Competition: The specificity of long-tail keywords means there's usually less competition for these terms, making it easier for smaller or niche websites to rank.

Higher Conversion Rates: Users searching with long-tail keywords often have a clearer intent, whether informational, transactional, or navigational, leading to higher conversion rates for websites that meet their specific needs.

Examples: "women's running shoe sale", "best books for teenagers 2024", "organic olive oil online".

Importance in SEO and Content Strategy

SEO Strategy: Incorporating both long-tail and short-tail keywords in your SEO strategy can help balance the volume of traffic with the quality of traffic. Short-tail keywords help increase visibility and brand awareness due to their high search volume, while long-tail keywords drive targeted traffic that is more likely to convert.

Content Strategy: A well-rounded content strategy utilises long-tail keywords to address specific queries and needs of your target audience, providing detailed, relevant content. Short-tail keywords can be used to structure broader topics and categories, serving as pillars around which more detailed content (targeting long-tail keywords) can be built.

In summary, the choice between targeting long-tail or short-tail keywords should be influenced by your website's goals, the nature of your products or services, and the level of competition in your sector. A balanced approach that includes both types of keywords is often the most effective strategy for achieving both broad visibility and attracting targeted, high-converting traffic.

3. On-Page SEO

3.1. Importance of title tags, meta descriptions, and header tags

Title tags, meta descriptions, and header tags are essential elements of SEO, playing a crucial role in influencing both search engine rankings and user engagement. Here's a detailed look at the importance of each component:

Title Tags

SEO Impact: Title tags are one of the most critical SEO elements. They provide search engines with primary context about the content of the page. Well-optimised title tags are key to improving your page's ranking for specific keywords.

User Engagement: The title tag is the first detail users see in search engine results pages (SERPs). An enticing and relevant title can significantly increase the click-through rate (CTR), drawing more visitors to your website.

Best Practices: Keep title tags under 60 characters to ensure they display fully in SERPs. Include main keywords towards the beginning and ensure the title is relevant to the page content.

Meta Descriptions

Influence on User Behaviour: Although meta descriptions do not directly influence rankings, they are critical in attracting users from the SERP. A well-crafted meta description acts as marketing copy for your webpage, influencing whether users decide to click through to your site.

CTR Optimisation: Effective meta descriptions provide a clear and enticing summary of the webpage content, incorporating relevant keywords and a call to action, encouraging users to click on the link.

Best Practices: Keep meta descriptions between 150-160 characters to prevent them from being cut off in SERPs. Ensure they accurately reflect the content of the page and include targeted keywords.

Header Tags (H1, H2, H3, etc.)

Structural SEO: Header tags help organise content on a page for better readability and user experience. They also provide structure for the content, making it easier for search engines to understand the main and subsidiary topics on a page.

Keyword Optimisation: Including relevant keywords in header tags, especially the H1, can help reinforce the page's relevance to specific search queries, supporting the page's SEO.

User Experience: Proper use of header tags can greatly enhance the readability of content, making it easier for users to scan through and find information that is relevant to them, thereby improving user engagement and retention.

Integration in SEO Strategy

Integrating well-optimised title tags, meta descriptions, and header tags into your SEO strategy enhances not only your visibility in search engines but also improves the attractiveness of your listings in search results. This integration can lead to higher organic traffic, better user engagement and, ultimately, increased conversions. These elements work collectively to communicate a cohesive and detailed understanding of your webpage's content to both search engines and potential visitors, making them indispensable tools in any robust SEO strategy and toolkit.

3.2. Strategies for optimising content for readers and search engines (keyword density, readability, etc.)

Optimising content for both search engines and readers involves a delicate balance. Effective content optimisation strategies ensure that the content is readable and engaging for users while also structured in a way that search engines can understand and rank it highly. Here are key strategies for achieving this balance:

1. Keyword Optimisation

Keyword Placement: Place your primary keywords in strategic locations such as the title tag, meta description, headers, and early in the content to emphasise their importance.

Keyword Density: Maintain a natural flow in the content by using keywords appropriately and avoiding over-optimisation. A generally recommended keyword density is around 1-2%, ensuring the text remains user-friendly while being effective for SEO.

Use of Related Keywords: Incorporate LSI (Latent Semantic Indexing - an indexing and retrieval method that uses a mathematical technique called singular value decomposition to identify patterns in the relationships between the terms and concepts contained in an unstructured text) keywords and synonyms to enhance content relevancy and avoid repetitive keyword usage, which can improve the content's comprehensibility and SEO.

2. Content Quality and Relevance

In-depth and Valuable Content: Provide comprehensive information that addresses the needs and questions of your audience. High-quality content that adds value encourages longer page visits and higher engagement.

Update Existing Content: Regularly update older posts with current information, new data, and improved keywords to keep them relevant and competitive in search rankings.

3. Readability

Clear Structure: Use headers (H1, H2, H3) to structure your content effectively. This not only helps with SEO but also makes your content easier to scan and digest for readers.

Short Paragraphs: Keep paragraphs short and concise. Aim for 2-3 sentences per paragraph to improve readability and keep the audience engaged.

Bullet Points and Lists: Utilise bullet points or numbered lists to break down complex information, making it more accessible and easier to understand.

4. Engaging and Attractive Format

Use of Images and Videos: Integrate relevant images, infographics, and videos to break text monotony, explain complex concepts visually, and enhance user engagement.

Bold and Italics: Emphasise important points using bold or italics sparingly to draw the reader's attention to key information.

5. Mobile Optimisation

Responsive Design: Ensure your content displays well on mobile devices. A mobile-friendly website improves the user experience and boosts SEO as search engines prefer mobile-optimised sites.

Fast Loading Speeds: Optimise media files and utilise modern coding practices to improve page loading times, crucial for both SEO and user experience.

6. Meta Tags and Descriptions

Meta Descriptions: Write compelling meta descriptions that include primary keywords. A well-crafted meta description can improve click-through rates from search engine results pages.

Alt Text for Images: Include descriptive alt text for images, incorporating keywords where appropriate. This improves image discoverability via search engines and aids accessibility.

7. Internal Linking

Connect Content: Use internal links to guide users to related content within your site. This increases time on site, reduces bounce rates, and helps distribute page authority throughout your website.

8. Social Sharing

Social Media Integration: Include social sharing buttons and encourage readers to share content. Social signals can indirectly influence SEO and help in driving additional traffic.

By following these strategies, you can create content that satisfies the needs of both search engines and your target audience, leading to better SEO performance and increased user engagement.

3.3. Image Optimisation (ALT text, file naming, compression)

Image optimisation is an essential part of enhancing website performance and search engine optimisation (SEO). It ensures that images contribute positively to page loading speeds, user engagement, and search engine rankings. Here are key strategies for optimising images effectively:

1. ALT Text

Purpose: ALT text (alternative text) describes an image's content and function on a webpage. It is crucial for web accessibility, allowing screen readers to describe images to visually impaired users.

SEO Benefit: ALT text also helps search engines understand the image content, which can contribute to SEO performance, especially in image search results.

Best Practice:

- Be descriptive and concise.
- Include relevant keywords naturally, when applicable.
- Avoid stuffing keywords as it can be penalised by search engines.

2. File Naming

Importance: Descriptive and keyword-rich file names help search engines understand what the image is about before even looking at the surrounding text or ALT text.

Best Practice:

- Use plain language and include keywords that reflect the image content.
- Separate words with hyphens rather than underscores (e.g., summer-beach-sunset.jpg).
- Keep file names relevant to the image and avoid generic names like IMG_12345.jpg.

3. Image Compression

Purpose: Reducing the file size of images without significantly compromising quality to improve page load times. Faster loading pages provide a better user experience and are favoured by search engines.

Tools:

- Online Tools: TinyPNG, Compressor.io, and Squoosh are user-friendly web tools for compressing both PNG and JPEG files.
- Software: Adobe Photoshop, GIMP, and other image editing software often offer options to adjust image quality and file size during the save process.
- WordPress Plugins: If using WordPress, plugins like Smush, EWWW Image Optimiser, or ShortPixel can automatically compress images as they are uploaded.

Best Practice:

- Balance between file size and image quality. Aim for the lowest file size while keeping the image visually appealing.
- Consider the format: JPEG is best for photographs with lots of colours, PNG is better for images with transparency, and SVG is ideal for logos and icons.

4. Image Dimensions

Sizing: Scale images to the size they will be displayed on your website. Oversised images take longer to load and consume more bandwidth.

Responsive Images: Use HTML's srcset attribute to serve different sized images based on the device screen dimensions, improving loading times on mobile devices.

5. Lazy Loading

Functionality: Lazy loading defers the loading of images until they are about to enter the viewport. This means images are loaded only as needed when the user scrolls down the page, reducing initial page load time.

Implementation: It can be implemented via attributes in HTML5 (loading="lazy") or through various JavaScript libraries.

By applying the above image optimisation strategies, you can significantly improve your site's performance and SEO, enhancing both the user experience and your site's visibility in search engine results.

3.4. URL structure and navigation

Effective SEO often involves fine-tuning many aspects of a website, with URL structure and site navigation being critical components. Optimising these elements can significantly influence how both users and search engines perceive and interact with your website. Here's how to optimise URL structure and navigation for better SEO:

Optimising URL Structure

Keep URLs Simple and Readable: URLs should be easy for both users and search engines to understand. Use clear, logical wording that conveys the content of the page. Avoid long URLs with unnecessary parameters or numbers.

Use Keywords: Include relevant keywords in URLs to help search engines understand what the page is about. This can also benefit users by providing a clear idea of the link's destination before they click on it.

Use Hyphens to Separate Words: Use hyphens (-) rather than underscores (_) to separate words in a URL. Search engines like Google treat hyphens as space but do not recognise underscores as separators, which can affect how they interpret the words.

Follow a Hierarchical Structure: If your website has multiple pages and categories, structure your URLs to reflect this hierarchy. This helps search engines understand the relationships between different pages and can enhance site indexing.

Example: https://examplewebsite.com/men/tops/t-shirts rather than https://examplewebsite.com /item12345

Keep URLs Consistent: Use consistent URL structures across your website. This not only helps with site organisation and user navigation but also aids in maintaining link equity when updating or restructuring your website.

Avoid Excessive Parameters: URLs with many parameters (e.g. ?id=123&session=456) can look like spam and reduce user trust. They can also cause issues with duplicate content. When parameters are necessary, use them sparingly and consider implementing canonical tags to avoid duplicate content issues.

Optimising Navigation

Logical Structure: Your website navigation should be logical and easy to follow. Organise content in a clear hierarchy and use category labels that make sense to the user. This structure helps search engines understand your site's architecture and index content more effectively.

Breadcrumbs: Implement breadcrumb navigation to enhance the user experience and bolster SEO. Breadcrumbs show users their current location within the site hierarchy and make it easy to navigate back to previous sections.

Example: Home > Men > Tops > T-shirts

Link Internally: Use internal links to help users easily find related content and to help search engines discover new pages. Internal linking also helps distribute page authority throughout your site, which can improve the SEO performance of individual pages.

Mobile-Friendly Navigation: Ensure that your navigation is easily usable on mobile devices. This can involve using a responsive design or a dedicated mobile menu. With mobile-first indexing, Google, predominantly, uses the mobile version of the content for indexing and ranking.

Navigation and Accessibility: Make sure your site's navigation is accessible to all users, including those with disabilities. Use proper HTML structure and attributes to ensure navigational elements are recognised and usable by assistive technologies.

Sitemaps: Utilise XML sitemaps to help search engines quickly find and crawl all the important pages of your site. Although sitemaps don't affect rankings directly, they can help improve the crawling of your site, ensuring more of your content is indexed.

By optimising your URL structure and navigation, you can enhance both user experience and SEO performance, leading to higher site engagement and improved search engine rankings. These improvements help users and search engines navigate your site more effectively, boosting your site's visibility and accessibility.

3.5. Mobile Optimisation and the importance of responsive design

Mobile optimisation and responsive design are crucial elements in modern SEO, especially since Google switched to mobile-first indexing in July 2019. This change means that Google predominantly uses the mobile version of a website's content for indexing and ranking, emphasising the importance of mobile-friendly web design. Here's how mobile optimisation and responsive design impact SEO and why they are vital:

Importance of Mobile Optimisation

User Experience (UX): A significant portion of internet traffic comes from mobile devices. Websites optimised for mobile provide a better user experience, reducing bounce rates and increasing time on site—both important ranking factors for SEO.

Increased Traffic and Visibility: Mobile-optimised sites are favoured in search results when users search on mobile devices. Given the high volume of mobile searches, having a mobile-friendly website can significantly increase your site's visibility and traffic.

Google's Mobile-First Indexing: With mobile-first indexing, Google primarily uses the mobile version of content for indexing and ranking. A website that isn't optimised for mobile may have lower rankings in search results, as the search engine may find the content less accessible or relevant to mobile users.

Responsive Design and Its SEO Benefits

Flexibility Across Devices: Responsive design uses a single URL and the same HTML code that adjusts to screen size, whether on a desktop, tablet, or smartphone. This flexibility improves user experience across all devices.

Avoids Duplicate Content: Having separate mobile and desktop sites can lead to duplicate content issues, which can negatively impact SEO. Responsive design eliminates this risk by having one URL and the same content across devices.

Improves Site Speed: Responsive websites often load faster on mobile devices than their non-responsive counterparts. Site speed is a ranking factor for Google, and faster sites provide a better user experience.

Lower Maintenance Needs: Managing one responsive website is less cumbersome than managing separate versions for mobile and desktop. This streamlined approach means less time spent on maintenance and more time on improving the site's content and SEO.

Higher Link Equity: For sites that use separate mobile URLs, link equity (the SEO value of links) is diluted between the mobile and desktop versions. With responsive design, all links point to a single domain, concentrating the link equity, which can boost SEO performance.

Implementing Mobile Optimisation and Responsive Design

Use Responsive Web Design: Implement responsive web design principles to ensure your site automatically adjusts to fit the screen size of any device.

Optimise Page Speed: Use tools like Google PageSpeed Insights to identify and fix elements that slow down your mobile site, such as large images or slow-loading scripts.

Touch-Friendly Design: Ensure all page elements are easy to navigate using touch controls. Buttons and links should be sufficiently sized and spaced to accommodate finger tapping instead of mouse clicking.

Test Mobile Usability: Regularly use tools like Google's Mobile-Friendly Test to check if your pages are optimised well for mobile devices. This tool also identifies usability issues like small text and incompatible plugins.

In conclusion, optimising for mobile and implementing responsive design are not just best practices for user experience but are also critical for SEO success in a 'mobile-first' world. These strategies ensure that websites are prepared to meet the needs of modern users and search engines, thereby enhancing visibility and driving traffic effectively.

4. Technical SEO

4.1. Website speed optimisation (importance of fast loading times)

Website speed optimisation is a critical factor in SEO and overall website performance. The loading time of your website affects user experience, bounce rate, and search engine rankings. Here's a detailed look at why website speed is important and how it influences SEO:

Importance of Fast Loading Times

User Experience: Fast-loading websites provide a better user experience. Websites that load quickly are more likely to keep users engaged, reducing the likelihood of visitors leaving before the page fully loads (bounce rate). A positive user experience can lead to higher conversion rates and increased customer retention.

Search Engine Rankings: Google and other search engines consider page speed as a ranking factor. Faster websites are likely to rank higher in search engine results pages (SERPs) because they provide a better user experience. Google has explicitly mentioned speed as a critical component, especially since the introduction of the Page Experience update, which includes Core Web Vitals as ranking signals.

Mobile Optimisation: With the increasing use of mobile devices for internet browsing, mobile users expect quick loading times even on less reliable network connections. Optimising your website's speed is crucial for mobile SEO, as slow-loading sites can be particularly cumbersome on mobile devices.

Increased Traffic and Lower Bounce Rates: Websites that load faster typically experience lower bounce rates. Users are more likely to stay on the site and explore other pages, which can lead to increased page views and more opportunities for conversions.

Strategies for Optimising Website Speed

Optimise Images: Ensure that images are not larger than necessary, are in the right file format (JPEG for photos, PNG for graphics with fewer than 16 colours), and are compressed for the web.

Enable Compression: Use file compression software to reduce the size of CSS, HTML, and JavaScript files that are larger than 150 bytes.

Minimise CSS, JavaScript, and HTML: Remove unnecessary spaces, comments, and characters. Use tools like UglifyJS for JavaScript, CSSNano for CSS, and HTMLMinifier for HTML Optimisations.

Leverage Browser Caching: Set "expires" headers for resources that are static and only change infrequently, which tells browsers to load previously downloaded resources from local disk rather than over the network.

Improve Server Response Time: Look at the performance of your web server, and consider optimising your databases, upgrading your hosting (consider dedicated hosting or a more powerful VPS), or adjusting your web server's configuration.

Use a Content Delivery Network (CDN): CDNs distribute your content across multiple, geographically diverse servers, allowing users to download content from servers that are closer to them, speeding up loading times.

Optimise Rendering Path: Analyse and optimise the critical rendering path, which is the sequence of steps the browser goes through to convert the HTML, CSS, and JavaScript into pixels on the screen. This includes minimising critical resources, deferring their download, minimising the number of critical bytes, and shortening the critical path length.

Use Async and Defer: For JavaScript files, use "async" (if the scripts do not depend on each other) or "defer" (if scripts depend on each other or rely on scripts that executed in the exact order they were called) attributes to control how JavaScript files are loaded.

Regularly testing and monitoring your website's speed using tools like Google PageSpeed Insights, GTmetrix, or WebPageTest, can provide insights and recommendations specific to your website's performance issues. By prioritising website speed and making necessary adjustments, you can enhance both the user experience and SEO effectiveness, ultimately leading to better SERP rankings and increased traffic.

4.2. Secure sockets layer (SSL) and its impact on SEO

Secure Sockets Layer (SSL) plays a significant role in modern SEO strategies, as it directly impacts website security, user trust, and search engine rankings. Here's how SSL influences SEO and why it's essential for websites today:

What is SSL?

SSL (Secure Sockets Layer), or more accurately, its successor TLS (Transport Layer Security), is a security technology that creates an encrypted link between a web server and a browser. This ensures that all data passed between the web server and browsers remain private and integral. SSL is most commonly seen through the HTTPS protocol in the URL, indicating a secure connection.

Impact of SSL on SEO

Enhanced Security and Trust: SSL certificates secure a website by encrypting the data transmitted between users and the site, protecting against eavesdropping, tampering, and phishing. This enhanced security is crucial for user trust, especially for websites that handle sensitive information, such as e-commerce sites and online banking services. A visible padlock icon in the address bar, along with HTTPS, reassures users that their data is secure, which can increase their likelihood of engaging with the site.

Search Engine Ranking Boost: Google has confirmed that HTTPS is a ranking signal. Websites with SSL certificates may receive a rankings boost, albeit a slight one, as part of Google's push towards more secure websites across the internet. This change is part of Google's broader strategy to ensure a safe web browsing experience.

Improved Website Credibility and Authentication: SSL certificates also include authentication, which means that you can be sure that you are sending information to the right server and not to an imposter trying to steal your information. This level of authentication is critical for websites that need to maintain a reputable online presence.

Lower Bounce Rates: Websites without SSL certificates may trigger browser warnings, such as "Not Secure" alerts when users enter pages that require personal information. Such warnings can alarm users and potentially increase bounce rates, as visitors may decide to leave the site rather than risk their security.

Better Referral Data: Using HTTPS also preserves the security of referral information when traffic passes to an HTTPS site from a secure website. Without SSL, referral data is often stripped away, and the visit is classified as "direct traffic" in analytics programs, which can skew the accuracy of referral data.

Implementing SSL

Obtain an SSL Certificate: You can purchase an SSL certificate from a Certificate Authority (CA). Many web hosting providers also offer SSL certificates as part of their hosting packages, sometimes even for free (e.g., Let's Encrypt).

Proper Configuration: Ensure that your SSL certificate is correctly installed and configured. This includes setting up all website pages to load over HTTPS and not just pages that require sensitive information.

Redirects: Implement 301 redirects from HTTP to HTTPS URLs to retain search engine rankings. This step ensures that users and search engines are directed to the secure version of your site.

Update Internal Links: Update all internal links to use HTTPS to avoid redirect chains and ensure a seamless user experience.

Verify with Search Engines: Update your sitemap and register the HTTPS version of your site with Google Search Console and other webmaster tools.

By integrating SSL/TLS into your website, you enhance both security and SEO performance, contributing to a safer internet and improving your website's visibility and user engagement.

4.3. The role of XML sitemaps and robots.txt files

XML sitemaps and robots.txt files are essential tools in SEO that help search engines more effectively crawl and index a website's content. Understanding their roles and how to properly implement them can significantly improve a site's SEO performance by ensuring that search engines can easily access and understand the site's structure and content.

XML Sitemaps

Role in SEO

Facilitates Faster Indexing: An XML sitemap is essentially a roadmap of your website that leads Google to all your important pages. XML sitemaps can be particularly important for websites with large archives, new websites, or websites with few external links. It helps search engines discover and index these pages, ensuring they are considered for ranking.

Improves Crawling of Dynamic Pages: For websites that frequently add new content or for those with complex architectures or dynamic pages, an XML sitemap is crucial for ensuring that search engines can discover and index new pages as quickly as possible.

Prioritisation and Frequency: Through the XML sitemap, you can provide additional information to search engines about your web pages, such as the relative importance of pages and how frequently they are updated. This helps search engines prioritise their crawling efforts based on the perceived importance and freshness of the content.

Best Practice:

- Keep Your Sitemap Updated: Automatically update your XML sitemap whenever new content is added. Tools like Google Search Console can notify you if there are issues with your sitemap.
- Submit to Search Engines: After creating or updating your sitemap, submit it to search engine webmaster tools, like Google Search Console and Bing Webmaster Tools.
- Optimise Sitemap Size: If your sitemap is very large (i.e., containing thousands of URLs), consider breaking it into smaller sitemaps. This makes it easier for search engine bots to parse.

Robots.txt

Role in SEO

Controlling Crawler Access: The robots.txt file, located at the root of your site's domain (e.g., https://www.example.com/robots.txt), tells search engine bots which parts of your site they can or cannot crawl. By preventing search engines from crawling irrelevant or duplicate content, you can ensure that only high-quality content is indexed.

Prevent Resource Wastage: It helps save your website's crawl budget (the number of times a search engine bot will crawl your site within a given time frame) by preventing bots from crawling unimportant or similar pages. This optimisation ensures that the crawl budget is spent on indexing valuable, unique content.

Secure Content: While not a primary security measure, robots.txt can be used to discourage search engines from indexing sensitive files and directories. However, this should not be the only method to protect sensitive data as it can easily be ignored by malicious bots.

Best Practice:

- Specific Instructions: Use specific directives like "Allow" and "Disallow" to control the access of legitimate bots.
- Be Cautious: Incorrect usage of the "Disallow" directive can accidentally block important pages from being indexed.
- Transparency and Maintenance: Regularly review and update the robots.txt file to accommodate new content or changes in your site architecture.
- Use with Sitemaps: Mention the location of your sitemap(s) in your robots.txt file to help search engines find it more easily.

Together, XML sitemaps and robots.txt files play crucial roles in optimising a site's interaction with search engines. They guide search engines through your site, highlighting what should be indexed, and what should be ignored. Proper management of these tools helps improve site visibility, enhance indexing efficiency, and maintain site security, contributing positively to the site's overall SEO footprint.

4.4. Structured data mark-up and schema.org

Structured data mark-up and Schema.org play a pivotal role in SEO by helping search engines understand the content of a website and its context. This clarity allows search engines to display more informative results for users, known as rich snippets, which can enhance visibility and improve click-through rates. Here's an in-depth look at how structured data and Schema.org impact SEO:

What is Structured Data?

Structured data is a standardised format to provide information about a page and classify the page content. It uses a vocabulary that search engines understand, allowing them to identify specific types of information on web pages, such as products, reviews, and events.

Schema.org

Schema.org is a collaborative effort by Google, Bing, Yahoo!, and Yandex to create a common set of schemas for structured data mark-up on web pages. It provides a shared vocabulary that webmasters can use to mark up their pages in ways that can be understood by major search engines.

Impact on SEO

Enhanced Search Engine Results: By implementing structured data, you can enhance how your pages are displayed in the search engines by adding rich snippets. These snippets may include star ratings, pricing, availability, or breadcrumbs, which can make your listing more attractive and informative, potentially increasing click-through rates.

Improved Content Understanding: Structured data helps search engines understand the context of your content, not just the content itself. This understanding can lead to better classification and indexing of your site, which may improve relevance in search results.

Support for Voice Search: As voice search becomes more prevalent, structured data can help voice search technologies understand the content of your website, making it more likely that your information will be included in voice search results.

Increased Visibility for Specific Queries: Implementing Schema.org mark-up can help your site become more visible for specific queries, particularly those that trigger rich results. For example, recipes with proper mark-up often appear in both the standard search results and the rich recipe carousel in Google Search.

Types of Schema Mark-up

Product Schema: Marks up products with pricing, availability, and review ratings.

Local Business Schema: Helps to provide information such as address, phone number, and opening hours of a business.

Event Schema: For events, providing dates, times, and locations.

Review Schema: To mark-up reviews and ratings of products or services.

FAQ Schema: For FAQ pages, helping them appear as rich results in search.

Implementing Structured Data

Select Relevant Schema: Identify the most relevant schema.org types for your content. Not every type of content will have or need a schema.

Use Google's Structured Data Markup Helper: This tool can help generate the necessary JSON-LD code (recommended by Google for structured data) that needs to be inserted into the HTML of your webpage.

Test Your Implementation: Use tools like Google's Rich Results Test to verify that your structured data is implemented correctly and is eligible for rich snippets.

Monitor Performance: After implementing structured data, use Google Search Console to monitor how your pages perform in search results and see how users interact with your rich snippets.

By incorporating structured data and using Schema.org vocabularies, websites can significantly enhance their search engine visibility and user interaction. This strategic implementation not only benefits SEO but also aligns with providing a clearer, richer user experience.

5. Off-Page SEO

5.1. Building a backlink strategy (quality vs. quantity)

Building a robust backlink strategy is a cornerstone of search engine optimisation because links are a fundamental signal that search engines use to determine the quality and relevance of your website. A successful backlink strategy focuses on acquiring links that improve your site's authority and drive relevant traffic, rather than just increasing the number of links. Here's how to balance quality versus quantity in your backlink strategy:

Quality of Backlinks

Relevance: Links from websites that are relevant to your site's content are more beneficial. For instance, a link from a well-regarded health publication would be more valuable for a medical clinic's website than a link from a random tech blog.

Authority: Links from high-authority sites (e.g., established and respected publications or organisations in your industry) carry more weight and can significantly boost your site's credibility and rankings.

Trustworthiness: Sites that are recognised as trustworthy and secure (not associated with spam or unethical practices) enhance the value of the links they provide.

Context: A link that naturally fits within the context of a page's content is more effective than one randomly placed or forced. For example, a backlink that is integrated into a high-quality article related to your niche is far more beneficial than a standalone link on a sidebar or footer.

Quantity of Backlinks

Scaling Up: While quality should never be sacrificed for quantity, having a larger number of high-quality backlinks can amplify SEO results. More good-quality backlinks can lead to higher authority and improved rankings.

Diverse Sources: Acquiring backlinks from a wide range of trustworthy domains can help enhance your site's authority and protect against penalties associated with having links from a limited pool of domains.

Strategies for Building Quality Backlinks

Content Creation: Create high-quality, engaging, and original content that naturally attracts backlinks. This includes blog posts, infographics, research studies, and videos that provide value and are likely to be shared or referenced by others.

Guest Blogging: Write articles for reputable sites in your industry. This not only provides valuable backlinks but also helps you reach a broader audience.

Broken Link Building: Identify broken links on external websites that you can replace with relevant content from your own site.

Influencer Outreach: Engage with influencers in your industry to get your content shared or to garner endorsements that may include backlinks.

Public Relations: Leverage PR strategies to get coverage from media outlets and other publications that can provide high-quality links back to your site.

Competitor Analysis: Review your competitors' backlink profiles to identify potential linking opportunities. Tools like Ahrefs, SEMrush, or Majestic can help you analyse where their backlinks are coming from.

Monitoring and Managing Your Backlink Profile

Regular Audits: Use tools to regularly audit your backlink profile to assess the health of your links, identify potentially harmful links, and determine the effectiveness of your backlink strategy.

Disavow Bad Links: If you identify bad or toxic links, consider using Google's Disavow Tool to tell Google to ignore these links so they don't hurt your rankings.

Ultimately, a successful backlink strategy emphasises the quality of links over sheer quantity. Quality backlinks from reputable, relevant sources have a much more significant positive impact on SEO, helping to build your site's authority, increase rankings, and drive targeted traffic. Focusing on ethical and sustainable link-building practices will yield the best long-term results for your SEO efforts.

5.2. Local SEO and the importance of Google My Business

Local SEO is a critical strategy for businesses that operate on a regional basis, where ranking in local search results directly impacts foot traffic, sales, and visibility. One of the most powerful tools for enhancing local SEO is Google My Business (GMB), now known as Google Business Profile. Understanding and effectively utilising this tool can significantly boost a business's presence in local search results.

The Importance of Local SEO

Local SEO helps businesses promote their products and services to local customers at the exact time they're looking for them online. This is achieved through various tactics that help increase a business's visibility in local search results and on map applications, where potential customers are actively seeking out services or products.

Role of Google My Business in Local SEO

Google My Business is an essential platform for local SEO as it directly affects what information is displayed in Google's local search results and on Google Maps. Here are the key ways GMB influences local SEO:

Visibility: A well-optimised GMB listing appears in Google Maps and local search results, often in the "Local Pack" (the block of local business results that appears at the top of relevant searches). This enhances visibility and can drive more traffic to your website or physical location.

Accuracy of Information: GMB allows businesses to manage their online information, including the business name, address, phone number, business hours, and more. Keeping this information accurate and updated is crucial as it helps customers find and interact with your business easily.

Customer Interaction: GMB provides a platform for businesses to engage with customers through reviews and Q&A. Responding to reviews can improve engagement and customer trust. Positive reviews can also influence potential customers and improve local search rankings.

Insights and Analytics: Google provides insights through GMB that can help businesses understand how customers interact with their listing, including how they found the business, actions they took, and other valuable data.

Posting and Updates: Businesses can use GMB to post updates, offers, events, and news directly to their profile. This content appears in Google Search and Maps, helping to keep customers informed and engaged.

Strategies for Optimising Google My Business

To maximise the benefits of your Google My Business listing for local SEO, consider the following strategies:

Complete Every Section: Fill out every part of your GMB profile. The more complete your profile, the more likely it is to appear in the Local Pack. Include keywords relevant to your business in the business description and services sections to boost your SEO further.

Maintain Accuracy: Ensure your information is always current, particularly your business hours, address, and contact information. This helps avoid customer frustration and negative experiences.

Encourage Reviews: Actively encourage happy customers to leave positive reviews. High-quality, positive reviews can improve your business's visibility and increase the likelihood that a potential customer will visit your location.

Use High-Quality Images: Upload high-quality photos of your business, products, and services. This not only enhances your listing's appeal but also engages users more effectively.

Regularly Update Your Listing: Use the Posts feature on GMB to keep your customers updated about anything new and to keep your profile active and relevant. Regular updates can signal to Google that your business is active, which can be beneficial for your SEO.

Manage and Respond to Reviews: Actively manage your reviews and respond to them, showing that you value customer feedback and engage with your clientele.

By effectively leveraging Google My Business, businesses can significantly enhance their local SEO, improving their visibility in local search results, attracting more local customers, and ultimately increasing their revenue.

5.3. Social media signals

Social media signals refer to the various interactions on social media platforms that relate to your brand, such as likes, shares, comments, and mentions. While social media signals do not directly influence search engine rankings in the same way that backlinks do, they play an important role in the broader scope of search engine optimisation (SEO). Here's how social media signals can impact SEO and why they are significant:

Indirect Impact on SEO

Increased Online Visibility and Traffic: Active social media profiles can drive traffic to your website through shared content and interactions. Increased traffic from social media can signal to search engines that your website is relevant and valuable, potentially improving your search rankings.

Enhanced Brand Recognition and Authority: Strong social media presence helps build brand recognition. Consistent interactions, quality content, and active engagement on social media platforms can enhance your brand's authority and reputation online. Search engines are increasingly sophisticated and can correlate brand strength and reputation with how it should rank in search results.

Content Distribution: Social media is an effective channel for promoting content. By sharing content links on social media, you increase the reach and visibility of your content, which can lead to more traffic and, potentially, more natural backlinks as your content is cited by other websites.

Longer Content Lifespan: Social media can help keep your content alive longer. As posts are shared and re-shared, they continue to attract attention and traffic over time, well beyond the initial publication date.

Keyword Strategy Alignment: Posts on social media can contribute to a brand's keyword strategy. Social media content, including descriptions, hashtags, and captions, indexed by search engines, can help these engines understand your brand's relevance to specific keywords.

Best Practices for Leveraging Social Media for SEO

Consistent Branding: Use consistent names, descriptions, and visuals across your social media profiles and your website to strengthen brand recognition.

Quality Content Creation: Create valuable, engaging, and shareable content that encourages interaction. More shares and interactions can lead to increased visibility and traffic.

Engage With Followers: Actively engage with users who interact with your posts. Respond to comments, participate in conversations, and encourage user-generated content.

Optimise Social Media Profiles: Make sure your social media profiles are fully optimised with up-to-date information, relevant keywords, and a clear link to your website.

Use Social Listening Tools: Monitor mentions of your brand and relevant conversations. This can provide insights into how your audience perceives your brand and help you tailor your content and SEO strategy accordingly.

Incorporate Social Sharing Buttons: Include social sharing buttons on your website's content to make it easy for visitors to share directly to their social media profiles. This increases the likelihood of receiving more social signals.

Promote Content Multiple Times: Due to the fleeting nature of social media feeds, consider promoting the same content multiple times, potentially in different formats, to maximise visibility and engagement.

While social media does not directly contribute to SEO rankings, its influence on brand presence, content distribution, and audience engagement plays a crucial role in a holistic SEO strategy. By fostering an active and engaging presence on social media, businesses can enhance their SEO indirectly and drive more organic traffic to their websites.

5.4. Strategies for earning inbound links through content marketing

Earning inbound links through content marketing is one of the most effective strategies for boosting your SEO. Inbound links, often referred to as backlinks, are links from external websites that point to your site. These are crucial because they signal to search engines that others vouch for your content, which can significantly enhance your site's credibility and ranking. Here's how to effectively earn inbound links through content marketing:

1. Create High-Quality, Shareable Content

Value and Relevance: Produce content that is informative, engaging, and valuable to your audience. High-quality content is more likely to be shared and linked to.

Types of Content: Invest in diverse formats such as blogs, infographics, videos, podcasts, and case studies. Different types appeal to different audiences and can be shared across various platforms.

2. Create Content That Attracts Links

Data-Driven Content: Original research, surveys, and data-rich studies are highly linkable because they provide authoritative information that others may reference in their own content.

'Linkbait' Pieces: Create compelling content specifically designed to attract links. This includes ultimate guides, top tips, in-depth tutorials, and thought leadership pieces that become go-to resources in your industry.

Visual Content: Infographics and interactive media can simplify complex data and are easily shareable, making them excellent for earning links.

3. Guest Blogging

Reputable Platforms: Write articles for reputable websites in your industry. This not only provides you with backlinks but also helps in reaching a broader audience.

Quality Over Quantity: Focus on writing for high-quality sites where your target audience spends time, rather than scattering your efforts across many lower-quality sites.

4. Use Strategic Content Formats

List Posts: Also known as "listicles," these posts are popular for their readability and shareability.

How-To Guides and Tutorials: These provide practical value to readers and are highly linkable because they help solve specific problems.

Resource Pages: Create useful resource lists and comprehensive industry guides. These can become reference points for others in your sector.

5. Promote Your Content

Social Media: Use social media platforms to share your content and reach a larger audience. The more it's seen, the more likely it will be linked.

Email Marketing: Send out newsletters that highlight compelling content to your subscribers who may link back to it.

Outreach: Conduct outreach campaigns to influencers and bloggers who might find your content valuable and might link back to it.

6. Build Relationships in Your Industry

Networking: Engage with other content creators, bloggers, and industry leaders. Relationships can lead to more organic links as your content is recognised and shared among industry peers.

Participation: Engage in community discussions, forums, webinars, and industry panels, and always look for opportunities to contribute.

7. Regularly Update Your Content

Refresh Old Content: Update your old posts with new data, links, and information. This can make your content relevant again and more likely to earn new links.

Repurpose Content: Turn existing content into new formats. For example, a popular blog post can be turned into a video tutorial.

By focusing on these strategies, you can create a strong content marketing approach that not only engages and retains your audience but also attracts valuable inbound links. These links are essential for improving your SEO, enhancing your online authority, and increasing your visibility in search engine results.

6. Content Strategy

6.1. Creating content that aligns with user intent

Creating content that aligns with user intent is pivotal in achieving effective SEO because it ensures that the content meets the needs and expectations of your audience, which is a key factor search engines consider when ranking pages. Understanding and catering to user intent can lead to higher engagement, improved satisfaction, and better search engine rankings. Here's how to align your content with user intent:

Understanding User Intent

User intent refers to the purpose behind a search query. Generally, user intent can be categorised into three main types:

Informational Intent: The user seeks information, such as answers to questions or details about a specific topic. The intent is to learn or understand something.

Navigational Intent: The user intends to visit a specific website or page. They are likely searching for a particular brand or website name.

Transactional Intent: The user is looking to make a purchase or engage in another type of online transaction. This could include any form of conversion, from subscribing to a service to buying a product.

Strategies for Aligning Content with User Intent

Keyword Research and Analysis:

Identify Intent: Use keyword research tools to help discern the intent behind the keywords. Look for clues in the keywords themselves—words like "buy," "price," "how to," "discount," or "what is" can signal the intent.

Analyse SERPs: Review the current search engine results pages (SERPs) for your target keywords to understand what type of content Google believes satisfies the searcher's intent.

Content Development Based on Intent:

Informational Content: Create blog posts, guides, infographics, and videos that provide valuable information or answer common questions related to your industry.

Navigational Content: Ensure your brand and product pages are optimised to help users who are searching specifically for what your brand offers. Include clear, concise, and compelling information about your products or services.

Transactional Content: Develop content that facilitates user transactions, such as product descriptions, reviews, and testimonials that support the purchasing decision. Ensure the inclusion of strong calls-to-action (CTA) and streamline the purchase process.

Optimising Content for User Intent:

Use Relevant Keywords: Incorporate keywords naturally into your content that align with the user's search intent. For transactional queries, include terms related to purchasing, deals, or sales.

Structure Your Content Appropriately: For informational content, use a clear and organised structure that makes it easy for users to find and absorb information. For transactional intents, focus on visibility of product features, benefits, and differentiators.

Enhance Readability and Accessibility: Make sure your content is easy to read and accessible on all devices, particularly on mobile.

Testing and Refinement:

User Feedback: Collect and analyse user feedback on your content to see if it's meeting their needs and expectations.

Performance Analysis: Use analytics to monitor how well your content performs in terms of traffic, engagement, and conversions. Look specifically at metrics like bounce rates, average time on page, and conversion rates to gauge whether the content aligns with user intent.

Continual Learning and Updating:

Stay Informed on Trends: User intent can evolve based on new industry developments or changes in search behaviour. Regularly update your content to reflect these changes.

Iterate Based on Results: Continuously refine your strategy based on what analytics reveal about your content's performance and relevance to user intent.

By focusing on user intent in your content strategy, you're more likely to create content that resonates with your audience, satisfies their search needs, and performs well in search engines. This approach not only helps with SEO but also enhances the overall user experience, fostering greater trust and engagement with your audience.

6.2. Importance of content freshness

Content freshness is a significant factor in SEO as it can influence how well your pages rank in search engine results. Search engines like Google aim to provide the most relevant and up-to-date information to users, so frequently updated content is often seen as more useful and relevant. Here's how content freshness impacts SEO and strategies to exploit it effectively:

Importance of Content Freshness in SEO

Relevance and Timeliness: Fresh content is typically more relevant, especially for rapidly changing topics or industries. Search engines prioritise content that is current because it is likely to be more valuable to users.

Increased Crawling Frequency: Websites that frequently update their content are often crawled more often by search engine bots. This regular crawling can lead to quicker indexing and improved rankings.

User Engagement: Fresh content can boost user engagement. Users are more likely to return to a website that consistently offers new and updated information, which can increase traffic and time spent on the site—both important signals in SEO.

Competitive Advantage: Regularly updated content can give you a competitive edge in search results, as it shows that your site is active and relevant. This is particularly important in industries where information changes quickly, such as technology, news, or entertainment.

Strategies for Leveraging Content Freshness

Regular Updates to Existing Content: Keep your existing content up-to-date by revising it regularly. This could involve updating statistics, adding new information, or revising outdated details. For example, annually updating a popular article can signal to search engines that the content remains relevant.

Adding New Content Regularly: Develop a content calendar to plan regular publications of new posts, articles, videos, or other content types. Consistency is key in keeping your website fresh.

News and Trends: Create content that taps into current events or trends related to your industry. This not only keeps your content fresh but also meets the immediate needs and interests of your audience.

Evergreen Content with Periodic Updates: Invest in evergreen content that remains relevant over time. Even evergreen content can benefit from occasional updates to ensure it stays comprehensive and complete.

User-Generated Content: Encourage user-generated content such as comments, reviews, or guest posts. This can provide a steady stream of fresh content without significant time investment from your end.

Repurposing Content: Take existing content and repurpose it into different formats. For example, turn a blog post into a video, an infographic, or a podcast episode. This approach not only refreshes the content but also appeals to different audience preferences.

Content Relevancy Layering: Add layers of relevance to older content by linking to more current content. This not only updates older pages but also creates a more interconnected content structure, improving the SEO performance of both new and old pages.

Monitoring Impact

Use Analytics: Monitor how updates affect your traffic, rankings, and engagement metrics. Tools like Google Analytics and Google Search Console can help you track changes and understand the impact of your content updates.

Feedback and Social Listening: Pay attention to user feedback and social signals. Comments, shares, and mentions can provide insights into how your audience perceives the freshness and relevance of your content.

Content freshness is not just about posting new content; it's about ensuring that all content on your website is current, relevant, and engaging. By implementing a strategy that prioritises content updates and freshness, you can improve your SEO, enhance user experience, and maintain a strong presence in search engine results.

6.3. Content types and formats that perform well in search

In SEO, not all content types and formats perform equally. The performance of content in search results can greatly vary depending on how well it aligns with user intent, how engaging it is, and how effectively it's optimised for search engines. Here's a breakdown of various content types and formats that tend to perform well in SEO, along with tips on how to optimise them:

1. Blog Posts

Performance: Well-written, comprehensive blog posts that provide valuable information can rank highly in search engines.

Optimisation Tips: Focus on a specific topic or keyword. Ensure the post is well-structured with headers, subheaders, and includes multimedia elements like images or videos to improve engagement and shareability.

2. Long-Form Articles

Performance: Long-form content often performs well because it provides in-depth information and tends to keep visitors on the page longer, which can signal quality to search engines.

Optimisation Tips: Cover topics thoroughly, use a clear structure, include authoritative sources, and update content regularly to keep it relevant.

3. Videos

Performance: Videos are highly engaging and can significantly increase the amount of time users spend on your site. They are also prominently displayed in video search results and can appear in the main Google search results.

Optimisation Tips: Host videos on your site or through a platform like YouTube. Ensure videos have SEO-friendly titles and descriptions, and consider adding subtitles and transcripts.

4. Infographics

Performance: Infographics can generate backlinks and social shares due to their visual appeal and ease of sharing.

Optimisation Tips: Include embed codes on your website, create compelling and easy-to-understand visuals, and ensure text elements are also presented as HTML text to be crawlable by search engines.

5. Product Pages

Performance: For e-commerce sites, optimised product pages can attract traffic from potential buyers searching for specific products.

Optimisation Tips: Use high-quality images, provide detailed product descriptions with keywords, include user reviews, and ensure the page loads quickly.

6. Listicles

Performance: Articles structured as lists (e.g., "Top 10...", "5 Best...") are popular because they are easy to read and often provide summarised, actionable information.

Optimisation Tips: Make your lists comprehensive and better than competing pages, use numbers in titles, and keep your lists updated.

7. How-To Guides and Tutorials

Performance: These types of content address specific questions or needs and provide step-by-step instructions, making them valuable for users.

Optimisation Tips: Use clear, concise, and descriptive headings; include step images or videos; and structure content with a logical progression.

8. Case Studies and Testimonials

Performance: Case studies and testimonials can perform well by demonstrating real-world applications of a product or service and building trust with potential customers.

Optimisation Tips: Tell a compelling story, include real data and results, and optimise for relevant keywords related to the industry or solutions provided.

9. Interactive Content

Performance: Quizzes, polls, and interactive tools can engage users more deeply than static content and can lead to higher retention on the site.

Optimisation Tips: Ensure interactive elements are mobile-friendly, load quickly, and are shared easily via social media.

10. eBooks and Whitepapers

Performance: These resources are valuable for generating leads, particularly in B2B sectors, and can help establish authority and expertise.

Optimisation Tips: Offer these in exchange for contact details, optimise landing pages for SEO, and promote through various channels including email and social media.

Incorporating a variety of these content types and formats into your SEO strategy can help attract and engage a broader audience, cater to different user preferences, and ultimately, improve your site's ranking in search results. Each type of content should be optimised based on best SEO practices and the specific preferences of your target audience.

7. SEO Tools and Analytics

7.1. Overview of essential SEO tools (e.g., Google Analytics, Google Search Console, SEMrush, Moz, Ahrefs)

A robust SEO strategy benefits greatly from a set of tools that provide insights into various aspects of website performance, from overall visibility in search engines to specifics like keyword rankings and backlink profiles. Here's an overview of essential SEO tools and what each offers:

1. Google Analytics

Purpose: Google Analytics primarily tracks and reports website traffic, giving insights into user behaviour, traffic sources, engagement metrics, and conversions.

Key Features:

- Real-time traffic analysis
- Audience demographics and behaviour tracking
- Conversion tracking
- Integration with Google Ads

Benefits: Helps understand how visitors interact with your website, which pages perform best, and where your traffic comes from.

2. Google Search Console

Purpose: Google Search Console is a tool set provided by Google that helps you understand your site's performance in Google search results and how Google views your site.

Key Features:

- Search performance analysis

- URL inspection tool
- Sitemap submission and status
- Mobile usability reports

Benefits: Vital for spotting issues such as crawl errors and security issues like hacking and malware. It also provides data on search queries, click-through rates, and Google's indexing of your site.

3. SEMrush

Purpose: SEMrush is a comprehensive SEO tool that provides data for SEO, PPC, social media, and content marketing campaigns.

Key Features:

- Keyword research and analytics
- Site audits
- Competitor analysis
- Social media tracking
- Rank tracking

Benefits: Offers extensive data on not just your own site's health and performance but also on competitors', providing insights into their strategies.

4. Moz

Purpose: Moz offers tools for keyword research, link building, site audits, and page optimisation insights, mainly focusing on improving search engine visibility.

Key Features:

- Keyword Explorer
- Rank Tracker
- Site Crawl
- Link Explorer

Benefits: Known for its Domain Authority and Page Authority metrics, Moz helps in assessing the strength of websites and their potential to rank in search engine results pages (SERPs).

5. Ahrefs

Purpose: Ahrefs is widely regarded as one of the best tools for backlink analysis, competitive analysis, URL rankings, keyword research, and more.

Key Features:

- Site Audit
- Backlink Checker
- Keyword Explorer
- Content Explorer

Benefits: Particularly strong in backlink and competitor analysis, Ahrefs provides detailed insights into where your competitors might be getting links and potential link-building opportunities.

How to Use These Tools in SEO

Regular Audits: Use tools like SEMrush, Moz, and Ahrefs for comprehensive audits of your site to identify SEO issues and areas for improvement.

Monitor Rankings: Track your keyword rankings with tools like Moz Rank Tracker or Ahrefs to see how well your pages are performing in SERPs.

Competitive Analysis: Utilise SEMrush and Ahrefs to understand your competitors' SEO strategies, including their top keywords, backlinks, and content marketing tactics.

On-Page Optimisation: Use insights from Google Search Console and Moz to optimise your pages for better rankings and visibility.

Link Building: Leverage the backlink data from Ahrefs and Moz to build and refine your link-building strategy.

Content Strategy: Use the keyword and content insights from these tools to guide your content marketing efforts.

Each tool provides unique capabilities that can help you fine-tune various aspects of your SEO strategy. Effective use of these tools in combination can provide a comprehensive view of your SEO health and identify potent strategies for improving your online presence.

7.2. How to measure and analyse SEO performance

Measuring and analysing SEO performance is essential to understand the effectiveness of your strategies and to make informed decisions for future Optimisations. Here are the key steps and tools involved in tracking and assessing the success of your SEO efforts:

1. Set Clear SEO Goals

Specific Objectives: Define what you want to achieve with your SEO efforts. This could be increasing organic traffic, improving rankings for specific keywords, enhancing click-through rates, or boosting conversions from organic search.

KPIs: Establish Key Performance Indicators (KPIs) that align with your goals, such as organic sessions, bounce rate, conversion rate, and keyword rankings.

2. Use the Right Tools

Google Analytics: Track overall website traffic, user behaviour, and conversions. It provides insights into which pages are performing well and where your traffic is coming from.

Google Search Console: Monitor your site's presence in Google SERPs. It helps you understand your site's search traffic and performance, fix issues, and make your site stand out in Google Search results.

SEO-specific tools like Ahrefs, SEMrush, or Moz: These tools offer deeper insights into backlink profiles, keyword rankings, and competitive analysis.

3. Track Keyword Rankings

Regular Monitoring: Keep track of how your keywords are ranking over time. This helps you understand if your SEO strategies are effective and how they are impacting your visibility in search engines.

Tools: Use tools like Ahrefs, SEMrush, or Moz to monitor keyword rankings. These tools can also help you discover new keywords and track competitors' keyword strategies.

4. Analyse Organic Traffic

Google Analytics: Analyse the amount of traffic coming from organic search. Look at trends over time, not just day-to-day fluctuations, to better understand long-term performance.

Segmentation: Break down the traffic to see which pages are driving performance and which are underperforming. Segment by device, geography, and type of visitor to further refine your strategy.

5. Evaluate Page Performance

Page-Level Analysis: Assess the performance of specific pages or sets of pages. Look at metrics like page views, time on page, bounce rates, and conversions.

Content Updates: Identify pages that need refreshment or more substantial updates based on their performance.

6. Measure Backlinks and Domain Authority

Backlink Tools: Use Ahrefs or Moz to track the number and quality of backlinks to your site. High-quality backlinks from reputable sites significantly boost SEO performance.

Domain Authority: Check changes in your domain authority over time to gauge the effectiveness of your link-building strategies.

7. Assess Conversions from Organic Traffic

Conversion Tracking in Google Analytics: Set up goals in Google Analytics to track how effectively organic traffic leads to desired actions, such as sales, sign-ups, or other conversions.

Attribution Models: Understand which interactions contribute most to conversions and assess the value of SEO in your marketing mix.

8. Monitor User Engagement

Engagement Metrics: Analyse metrics such as average session duration and pages per session to gauge how engaging your content is for users.

Bounce Rate: Evaluate bounce rates to understand if your content meets user expectations and is relevant to their search queries.

9. Report and Refine

Regular Reporting: Compile regular reports that track all these metrics against your KPIs. Use these reports to present findings to stakeholders or to revise strategies.

Continuous Improvement: SEO is an ongoing process. Use the insights from data to continually refine and enhance your SEO strategies.

By systematically measuring and analysing these aspects of your SEO performance, you can build a clearer picture of what's working, what isn't, and where you can improve. This approach not only helps justify SEO efforts but also guides future Optimisations and enhancements.

7.3. Setting up and understanding SEO KPIs

Setting up and understanding Key Performance Indicators (KPIs) is essential for tracking the effectiveness of your SEO strategies and ensuring that your efforts are aligned with your business objectives. KPIs help quantify your performance and provide actionable insights. Here's how to set up and understand SEO KPIs effectively:

1. Define Your SEO Goals

Start by clearly defining what you want to achieve with your SEO efforts. These goals will guide which KPIs are most relevant. Common SEO goals include:

- Increasing overall organic traffic.
- Improving rankings for specific keywords.
- Boosting conversion rates from organic traffic.
- Enhancing user engagement metrics like time on site and pages per session.
- Growing the number of high-quality backlinks.

2. Identify Relevant KPIs

Based on your goals, select KPIs that will provide you with insights into your SEO performance. Some of the most useful SEO KPIs include:

Organic Sessions: Tracks the number of visits to your site from organic search. It helps gauge the overall visibility and effectiveness of your SEO efforts.

Keyword Rankings: Monitors the rankings for specific keywords and tracks changes over time, providing insights into your content's SEO performance.

Conversion Rate: Measures the percentage of visitors who complete a desired action (like filling out a form, signing up for a newsletter, or making a purchase) divided by the total number of visitors.

Bounce Rate: The percentage of visitors who navigate away from the site after viewing only one page. A high bounce rate might indicate that the site content is not relevant to what the users were expecting.

Page Load Time: Affects user experience and SEO; faster pages are generally favoured in search engine rankings.

Backlinks: The total number and quality of backlinks pointing to your website. This is a critical factor in SEO as it boosts credibility and authority.

Click-Through Rate (CTR): The percentage of users who click on your site's listing in the search results. Improving CTR can be an indicator of effective meta descriptions and title tags.

3. Set Up Tracking Tools

Utilise tools that can help you track these KPIs effectively:

Google Analytics: For tracking organic sessions, bounce rate, conversion rate, and user engagement metrics.

Google Search Console: For insights into keyword rankings, CTR, and the health of your website (like indexing status and web errors).

SEO platforms like Ahrefs, SEMrush, or Moz: These tools are especially useful for detailed keyword tracking, backlink analysis, and competitive insights.

4. Regular Review and Reporting

Establish a Reporting Cycle: Decide how often you will review and report on these KPIs. For most businesses, a monthly review is sufficient, but some might require weekly checks depending on the dynamic nature of their industry.

Create Dashboards: Many tools allow you to create dashboards where you can visualise your KPIs in real-time. This can be helpful for keeping track of ongoing performance and trends.

5. Analyse and Optimise

Data Analysis: Regularly analyse your data to identify trends, successes, and areas needing improvement. Look for correlations between different KPIs to understand the broader impact of your SEO strategies.

Continuous Improvement: SEO is an ongoing process. Use the insights gained from your KPI tracking to refine and optimise your SEO strategies. For example, if certain keywords are performing well, you might expand your content in those areas.

6. Align with Business Objectives

Ensure that your SEO KPIs align with overall business objectives. This alignment helps demonstrate the value of SEO within the broader business context and ensures that your digital marketing efforts contribute to the company's goals.

By setting up and regularly reviewing these KPIs, you can closely monitor your SEO health, justify investments in SEO to stakeholders, and strategically steer your efforts to maximise ROI from your SEO initiatives.

8. SEO Trends and Future Directions

8.1. Voice search optimisation

Voice search optimisation is becoming increasingly important as more users adopt voice-activated devices, such as smartphones, smart speakers, and virtual assistants. Voice searches tend to be more conversational, longer, and often involve direct questions, which necessitates adjustments to traditional SEO strategies. Here's how to optimise your website for voice search:

1. Focus on Conversational Keywords

Long-tail Keywords: Since voice searches are more conversational (and easier to execute), they tend to be longer than text-based searches. Optimise for long-tail keywords that mimic how real people talk and ask questions.

Natural Language: Use natural, conversational language in your content. Think about how people speak naturally, and include these phrases in your SEO strategy.

2. Optimise for Question Keywords

Who, What, Where, When, Why, How: Many voice searches are question-based, looking for specific information. Create content that answers these questions directly. For instance, FAQ pages can be particularly effective for targeting these queries.

Featured Snippets: Google often pulls voice search answers from featured snippets. Structure your content to increase your chances of appearing in these snippets. Answer questions directly and succinctly at the beginning of your content.

3. Improve Local SEO

Local Queries: Voice search is commonly used for local information. Ensure your local SEO is strong by optimising for phrases like "near me" or "close by."

Google My Business: Keep your Google My Business listing up-to-date with accurate hours, location, and contact info to improve visibility in local voice search results.

4. Website Loading Speed

Speed Optimisation: Voice search devices, especially mobile ones, favour websites that load quickly. Ensure your website is optimised for speed by compressing images, using a responsive design, and minimising server response time.

5. Structured Data

Schema Markup: Use schema mark-up to help search engines understand the context of your content. This is especially helpful for voice search devices that rely on quick, accurate results for user queries.

6. Create Mobile-Friendly Content

Mobile Optimisation: Since many voice searches are done on mobile devices, ensure your website is mobile-friendly. This means a responsive design, fast loading times, and accessible navigation.

7. Useful, High-Quality Content

Content Depth: Provide comprehensive, authoritative content that meets users' needs and answers their questions. Detailed content that thoroughly covers a topic may rank better in voice search.

8. Security

HTTPS: Voice search devices, like all modern browsers and technologies, favour secure connections. Ensure your website uses HTTPS to improve both security and the likelihood of ranking well.

9. Test and Refine

Voice Search Analytics: If possible, analyse how people find your site through voice search and what queries they use. This can inform your content strategy to better align with voice search behaviour.

10. Accessibility

Clear Audio Options: For those using voice-driven devices due to accessibility reasons, ensure that your website offers content that is easy to understand when read aloud by a screen reader.

By incorporating these strategies into your SEO plan, you can better position your site to benefit from the growing use of voice search. As voice technology evolves and becomes more integrated into daily routines, being proactive in voice search optimisation will become even more crucial for maintaining and improving search engine visibility.

8.2. The impact of artificial intelligence and machine learning on search

The impact of artificial intelligence (AI) and machine learning (ML) on search engine optimisation (SEO) is profound and continually evolving. These technologies have significantly transformed how search engines understand and process content, user intent, and search queries. Here's an overview of how AI and ML are influencing SEO:

1. Improved Search Algorithms

Search Personalisation: AI and ML enable search engines to personalise search results based on user behaviour, search history, location, and other factors. This personalisation means that SEO strategies need to focus more on targeting user intent rather than just optimising for generic keywords.

Understanding Context: Machine learning algorithms, such as Google's RankBrain, help interpret the queries that people type into the search engine and determine what types of content are most likely to satisfy those queries. This has increased the importance of related keywords and semantic search optimisation.

2. Content Relevance and Quality

Content Evaluation: AI algorithms are increasingly capable of evaluating content quality and relevance to a specific search query. This goes beyond keyword presence to include factors like content depth, readability, structure, and originality. High-quality, well-researched content is more important than ever.

User Engagement Metrics: AI uses signals such as click-through rates, time spent on a page, bounce rates, and other engagement metrics to assess content quality. SEO strategies must now include optimising user experience and engagement.

3. Voice Search Optimisation

Natural Language Processing (NLP): AI advancements in NLP have led to improvements in voice recognition systems, making devices better at understanding human speech. This affects SEO as voice search queries tend to be longer and more conversational. Optimising for these types of queries necessitates a focus on natural language and question-based content.

4. Visual Search Technology

Image Recognition: AI improves how search engines interpret and index images, which affects how images appear in search results. Optimising images with accurate, descriptive file names and alt text is crucial. Furthermore, emerging visual search capabilities mean businesses need to consider how their products or services could be discovered through image searches.

5. Automated and Predictive SEO

Automation Tools: AI powers many SEO tools that help automate routine tasks like keyword research, content analysis, and even some on-page SEO Optimisations. These tools can predict the potential success of content and recommend adjustments based on projected trends.

Predictive Analysis: AI can analyse data and identify trends, helping marketers anticipate changes in user behaviour or search trends. This predictive capacity enables proactive adjustments to SEO strategies.

6. Search Engine Bots Evolve

Crawler Sophistication: AI and machine learning make search engine crawlers smarter, meaning they can better understand which parts of a website are most important and how frequently they should be crawled. This underscores the importance of having a well-structured, easily navigable website.

7. SEO Strategy Personalisation

Hyper-Personalisation: As AI gets better at understanding individual preferences, SEO strategies will need to become more personalised, tailoring content not just to general audience segments, but potentially to individual users.

8. Challenges and Opportunities

Constantly Changing Algorithms: One of the biggest challenges with AI in search, is the pace of change in algorithms. SEO professionals need to stay informed and quickly adapt to these changes.

Ethical Considerations: As AI capabilities grow, so do concerns about privacy, data security, and the ethical use of AI in manipulating search rankings or user behaviours.

Overall, AI and ML are making search engines much more intuitive and user-focused. For SEO professionals, this means adapting strategies to prioritise the user experience, leveraging AI-driven tools to enhance their work, and continuously learning to keep up with technological advancements.

8.3. Importance of user experience (UX) in SEO rankings

User Experience (UX) has become increasingly important in SEO rankings as search engines, like Google, continue to refine their algorithms to prioritise sites that offer the best experience to users. This shift recognises that user satisfaction is a critical component of a website's value, influencing metrics such as engagement, retention, and conversions. Here's a detailed look at why UX is vital for SEO:

1. Google's Core Web Vitals

Google has integrated specific user experience metrics into its ranking criteria, known as Core Web Vitals. These include:

Largest Contentful Paint (LCP): Measures loading performance. To provide a good user experience, LCP should occur within 2.5 seconds of when the page first starts loading.

First Input Delay (FID): Measures interactivity. Pages should have an FID of less than 100 milliseconds.

Cumulative Layout Shift (CLS): Measures visual stability. Pages should maintain a CLS of less than 0.1.

These metrics highlight the importance of a website's speed, responsiveness, and visual stability, which are key aspects of UX.

2. Mobile Optimisation

With the increase in mobile internet usage, Google has adopted a mobile-first indexing policy. This means that Google predominantly uses the mobile version of the content for indexing and ranking. A mobile-optimised site with responsive design ensures a good UX across all devices and is crucial for maintaining strong SEO rankings.

3. Improved Engagement Metrics

Good UX design helps improve user engagement metrics such as time on site, pages per session, and bounce rate. These metrics are indicative of the quality of experience users have on a site:

Time on Site: A longer time spent on a site often indicates that users find the content relevant and engaging.

Pages per Session: More pages per session can suggest that users are interested in exploring more content on the site.

Bounce Rate: A lower bounce rate might indicate that the site is meeting users' expectations and they are interested in the content beyond the initial landing page.

4. Enhanced Usability

UX focuses on making websites easy to use. A site that is simple to navigate, has a clear structure, and includes well-defined calls to action (CTAs) makes it easier for users to find what they are looking for. This not only improves user satisfaction but also helps search engine crawlers better understand and index the website.

5. Content Readability and Accessibility

Ensuring content is readable and accessible is a major part of UX. This includes using clear fonts, reasonable text sizes, sufficient colour contrast, and logical content layout. Accessible content is important not only for users with disabilities but for all users and is positively regarded by search engines.

6. Trust and Credibility

Websites that are professionally designed and provide a secure browsing experience (e.g., using HTTPS) are more likely to be trusted by users. Trust is a crucial factor in UX and influences SEO indirectly through increased user engagement and directly through metrics like conversion rates.

7. Reduced Bounce Rate

A good UX can significantly reduce the bounce rate as users are more likely to stay on a website that is easy to navigate, loads quickly, and displays well on their device. Search engines use bounce rate as an indicator of the quality and relevance of a site to a user's query.

Conclusion

Integrating UX into SEO strategies is no longer optional but essential. Search engines continue to advance their algorithms to favour websites that provide superior user experiences. Therefore, improving UX not only boosts SEO rankings but also supports business goals by enhancing user satisfaction and loyalty.

9. SEO Myths and Misconceptions

9.1. Common SEO myths debunked

Search Engine Optimisation (SEO) is a complex field riddled with myths and misconceptions. Here are some common SEO myths debunked:

Myth: More keywords mean better rankings.

Debunked: Known as "keyword stuffing," overloading content with keywords can actually harm your rankings. Search engines like Google prefer natural, user-friendly content. Overusing keywords can make text unreadable and may trigger penalties from search engines.

Myth: SEO is a one-time task.

Debunked: SEO requires ongoing effort. Search algorithms are constantly updated, competitors change their strategies, and new content needs optimisation. Regular updates, content improvements, and strategy adjustments are essential for maintaining or improving rankings.

Myth: Links are all that matter in SEO.

Debunked: While backlinks from reputable sites are important, they're just one part of SEO. High-quality content, user experience, site speed, mobile responsiveness, and technical SEO factors also significantly impact rankings.

Myth: Social media doesn't impact SEO.

Debunked: Social signals such as likes, shares, and visibility can indirectly influence SEO. They increase content distribution, which can lead to more backlinks and branded searches, both of which are beneficial for SEO.

Myth: Higher traffic equals higher rankings.

Debunked: Traffic volume doesn't directly influence rankings. Search engines focus more on relevance and user satisfaction. High traffic with poor engagement or high bounce rates might not lead to better rankings.

Myth: HTTPS is not necessary for ranking.

Debunked: Google has confirmed that HTTPS, which ensures a secure connection, is a ranking factor. Websites not using HTTPS may be penalised or flagged as insecure, potentially decreasing user trust and engagement.

Myth: Meta tags don't matter.

Debunked: While meta keywords are no longer relevant, other meta tags like the title tag and meta description still play critical roles in SEO. They influence click-through rates from the search engine results page (SERP), which can impact rankings.

Understanding these misconceptions can help you focus on what truly matters in SEO: creating valuable content, enhancing user experience, and using ethical practices to improve and sustain your search engine rankings.

9.2. Black hat vs. white hat SEO practices

In the world of Search Engine Optimisation, tactics are typically divided into two main categories: "white hat" and "black hat." These terms, borrowed from Wild West (cowboy) films where the hero wears a white hat and the villain wears a black hat, help differentiate between ethical and unethical SEO practices. Understanding these distinctions is essential for maintaining the integrity and effectiveness of your SEO strategy.

White Hat SEO

White hat SEO refers to the use of optimisation strategies, techniques, and tactics that focus on a human audience opposed to search engines and completely follow search engine rules and policies. Here are some characteristics and examples of white hat SEO:

Content Quality: Creating high-quality content that is original, useful, and informative. This involves thorough research, fact-checking, and editing to provide significant value to users.

Keyword Use: Implementing keywords naturally and in context. Keywords should enhance the content rather than detract from its readability or relevance.

User Experience (UX): Designing a website that is easy to navigate, loads quickly, and is accessible to all users, including those with disabilities.

Organic Link Building: Earning links from reputable sites without manipulative tactics. This could involve guest blogging, creating shareable infographics, or producing compelling content that naturally attracts backlinks.

Mobile Optimisation: Ensuring the site is mobile-friendly, considering the increasing number of users accessing the internet via smartphones and tablets.

Black Hat SEO

Black hat SEO consists of practices that are used to increase a site or page's rank in search engines through means that violate the search engines' terms of service. The use of black hat techniques can lead to severe penalties from search engines, including being completely banned from search results. Here are some examples of black hat SEO:

Keyword Stuffing: Overloading webpages with keywords in an unnatural way, hoping to manipulate a site's ranking.

Cloaking: Presenting different content or URLs to users and search engines. Users see one type of content while search engines are presented with another, typically to trick search engines to rank the content higher.

Hidden Text or Links: Hiding text or links within your website's code to manipulate Google's indexing algorithms. This can be done by using text the same colour as the background or setting the font size to zero.

Link Farms: Participating in communities where every website links to every other website with the sole intention of artificially increasing link popularity.

Doorway Pages: Creating low-quality webpages that are loaded with keywords and phrases but are invisible to the user and redirect to the actual page.

The Consequences

Using black hat SEO tactics can produce quick gains in terms of rankings, but these are usually short-lived. Search engines are continuously updating their algorithms to catch deceptive techniques and will penalise sites found to be using such practices, often by reducing their rankings or removing them from search results altogether.

Conversely, white hat SEO strategies are designed to produce lasting results. By focusing on the user experience and adhering to search engine guidelines, websites can achieve sustainable rankings, improve user engagement, and build trust with their audience.

10. Conclusion

It is important to recognise that Search Engine Optimisation is not just a set of technical directives, but a fundamental component of your digital marketing strategy. Throughout this book, we've explored the multiple facets of SEO—from understanding how search engines work and the importance of keywords, to the nuances of technical SEO, content strategies, and the significance of mobile optimisation and user experience.

We started by laying the groundwork with the basics of SEO, where we explained how search engines operate and the critical role of keywords. As we progressed, we delved deeper into on-page and off-page SEO techniques, emphasising the balance between optimising for search engines and crafting content that resonates with your audience. **The importance of high-quality, relevant content cannot be overstated**; it remains at the heart of successful SEO strategies.

Technical SEO presented us with the tools and knowledge to ensure that search engines can crawl, understand, and index websites efficiently. From the structure of your URLs to the responsiveness of your design and the speed of your pages, every element of your website counts towards building a solid foundation that enhances both user experience and search engine visibility.

Mobile optimisation's role in SEO highlighted the shift towards a mobile-first approach, reflecting changes in user behaviour and Google's indexing practices. Ensuring that your site performs flawlessly on a variety of devices is now indispensable, as more users access the internet via smartphones and tablets than ever before.

We also discussed the transformative impact of artificial intelligence and machine learning on SEO. These technologies are not just changing how search engines rank content, but also how SEO strategies are planned and implemented. Staying updated with these advancements will keep you ahead of the game in terms of SEO.

Social media's indirect influence on SEO through engagement and visibility and the emerging significance of voice search optimisation have opened new avenues for reaching audiences. These trends underscore the need to continuously adapt and innovate your strategies to align with how content is being consumed today.

Finally, we have emphasised that SEO is an ongoing process. The digital landscape is constantly changing, and staying informed through continuous learning and adapting is critical. Regularly monitoring your website's performance using the tools and techniques discussed will help you refine your strategies and maintain your competitive edge.

In essence, the key to mastering SEO lies in understanding the balance between technological optimisation and human-centred content creation. As you apply these insights, remember that SEO is about being more visible, more engaging, and more relevant to the needs of your audience. With patience, persistence, and perseverance, the information outlined in this book will guide you to SEO success, enhancing both your website's performance and your organisation's growth.

www.ingramcontent.com/pod-product-compliance
Lightning Source LLC
LaVergne TN
LVHW081805050326
832903LV00027B/2106